LEARN TO DRAW
NOW!

by D. C. DuBosque

PEEL
PRODUCTIONS

For my father, who taught me many of the "tricks" of drawing, and my mother, who found answers to "Mommy, what should I draw?'

Published by Peel Productions
P.O. Box 185, Molalla, OR 97038

Manufactured in the United States of America

10   9   8   7   6   5   4   3   2

Library of Congress Cataloging-in-publication data

DuBosque, D. C.
        Learn to draw now! / by D. C. DuBosque
                p.   cm. — (Learn to draw)
        Summary: Introduces techniques and exercises for rendering the basic three-dimensional forms essential for realistic drawing: the cylinder, cone, sphere, and box.
        ISBN 0-939217-16-3
        1. Drawing—Study and teaching (Elementary)—Juvenile literature.
        [1. Drawing—Technique.] I. Title. II. Series.
        NC630.D8 1991
        741.2'4—dc20   90-27879

Contents

· ·

Before you start:
a note from the author

Most people think there's something mysterious about drawing—that somehow you either "can" draw or you "can't" draw. Most people never have thought that maybe you learn to draw the same way you learn to ride a bicycle, or write the letters of the alphabet. It doesn't occur to them that maybe you **don't** have to have a special gift to draw, that maybe you just have to **practice**.

In this book you'll look at, and draw, simple three-dimensional forms. There's nothing here for you to look at and say, "Wow, I wish I could draw like that." Everything here is for you to look at, try, and then say, "I **know** how to draw that!"

As you go through this book, remember that learning to ride a bicycle involves—for most people—falling off once or twice (or more!), and that learning anything, whether the alphabet or a new language, involves mistakes. They're part of learning. Sometimes mistakes are funny; sometimes they're not. But where there's learning, you'll find mistakes, and that's certainly true in drawing. It's important to just keep looking, and practicing—ask any artist or illustrator!

So grab a pencil and paper and let's begin! And if, as you look and draw, you have ideas about how to make this—or future drawing books—more helpful, please write to me care of the publisher (address on page 64). Happy drawing!

Doug Dubosque

LEARN TO DRAW **NOW!**

The Good News

The good news about the exercises in this book is that you don't need anything fancy to do them. In fact all you need is:

Plain old pencils—#1 are best.

Recycled Paper—start collecting practice paper, if you don't already. The supply is endless. Anywhere there's a computer printer or a photocopier, you can be sure people are wasting tremendous amounts of paper. You may be able to use the back sides for practice drawings. Keep plenty handy.

Pencil sharpener—keep nearby. Use as often as you need to.

Eraser—don't plan to use it very much. This is a book about **drawing**, not **erasing**. Save your eraser for the next book, which will be called *Learn To Erase NOW!*

Just kidding.

For best results, use a pencil to do the drawings in this book. Because pencils are not all the same, and paper is not all the same, do a test strip before you start - a gray scale to see how dark and how light you can draw:

(This is great practice—when you can't think of anything to draw, make gray scales!)

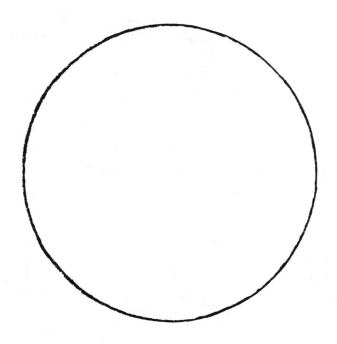

Part 1

· ·

Mysteries Revealed:
when round is not round

Let's start with a little quiz.
Here's a drawing of something. What is it?

(The sun? The moon? A coin?)

Here's another view of the **same** object. What is it?

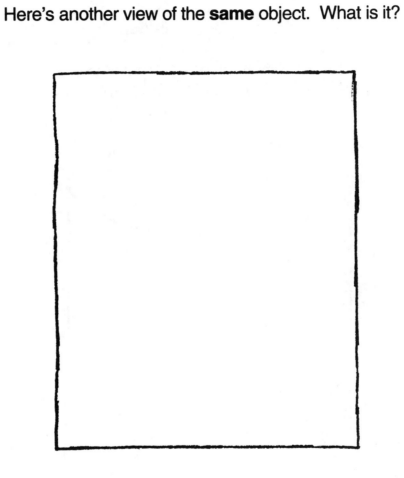

Answer: it's a **cylinder**.

Take a minute to look around you —
can you see any *cylinders*?

When you look at a cylinder from the round end,
you see a circle.

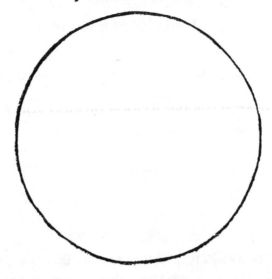

When you look at a cylinder from the side,
you see a rectangle.

But what do you see when you look at the cylinder from a
different angle?

You see an **ellipse**. It's not the circle you see when you look at a cylinder from the top. It's not the straight line you see when you look at a cylinder from the side.

This is an **ellipse**. Notice how the curved line of the ellipse gets smaller and smaller at each end—but it never comes to a point!

An ellipse is what you see when you look at a circle from an angle. It only looks round if you're precisely, perfectly, *exactly* in front of it—which you almost never are. Otherwise, what you're really seeing is an ellipse.

Right now, take a look around you—do you see any ellipses? Is there a "round" clock in the room? Is there a "round" trash can, or a cylindrical container like a can or a cup? What other "round" objects are there in the room that you actually see as ellipses?

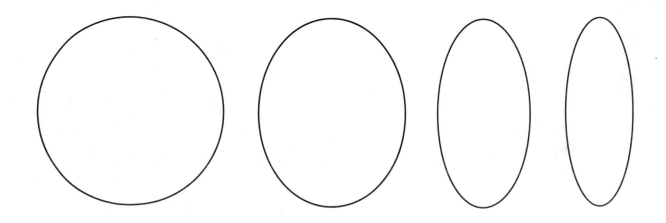

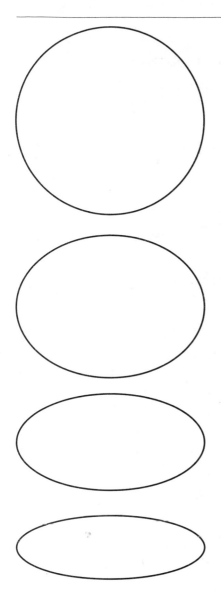

Ellipses come in different shapes. There are wide ellipses, which look almost like circles, and thin ellipses, which look like circles that have been flattened. The closer you are to being precisely, perfectly, *exactly* in front of a circle, the wider the ellipse will be. When you're off to the side of a circle, the ellipse will be thinner. The circle looks different, depending on whether you're right in front of it, or off to the side.

You can see a progression of ellipses on this page—from wide to thin (and back again, depending on which way you move your eyes!) Imagine you're holding a coin, or a phonograph record, or a compact disc in your hand, slowly turning it—can you see how it would look like the ellipses on this page as it turned?

If the circle had other circles inside of it, like the grooves of a phonograph record, those circles would also turn into ellipses, exactly as wide or thin as the biggest circle— but, of course, on a smaller scale.

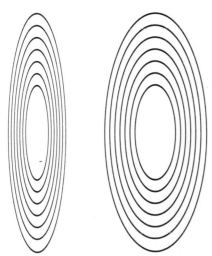
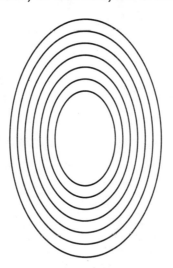
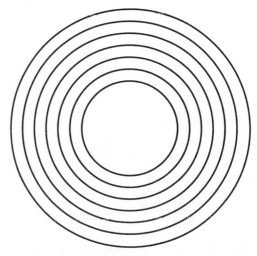

Now: there is one rule you need to know about ellipses: no matter how thin an ellipse becomes, it never comes to a point at the ends. The ends are always a little bit round!

This is what you want your ellipse to look like:

This is what you **don't** want your ellipse to look like:

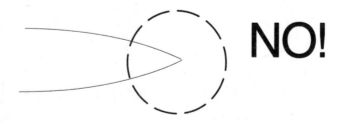

So you see, sometimes "round" is not round: let's try drawing some ellipses. You probably won't be an expert right away—like anything new, this may take a few tries, and then a little practice before you are able to it well. Use your pencil, any old piece of paper, and start drawing very *lightly!*

There are different ways to draw ellipses. You can go over and over, as fast or slow as you please, until the shape looks right. Or, you might prefer drawing little bits that connect together. Artists use both techniques. What's important is to end up with an ellipse, because you'll use it again and again!

How does your ellipse look? Did you make any mistakes? If you did, don't be discouraged. It means you are learning. Keep trying!

Strategy #1

· ·

When you start drawing, always start out very lightly. This way, when things don't work exactly right, nobody will notice. Better still: you'll have a chance to correct your mistake without having to start over, and without wasting a piece of paper!

Once you feel confident that you can draw an ellipse (by now you may even feel like an ellipse expert), turn your paper over (or do what I do, and use a fresh sheet of recycled paper) and draw a medium-size ellipse towards the top of your page.

Now you need to be an ellipse expert (or at least pretty comfortable drawing ellipses), because the next step is to draw another ellipse exactly like the first one—and directly below it. Your drawing should look like this, more or less:

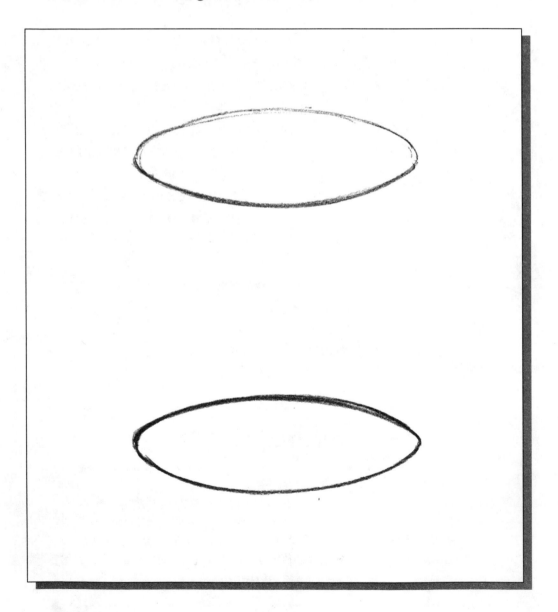

Now turn your paper sideways (it makes it easier to draw this part) and lightly connect the very outside end of your ellipses. Don't use a ruler - you need practice drawing straight lines without one.

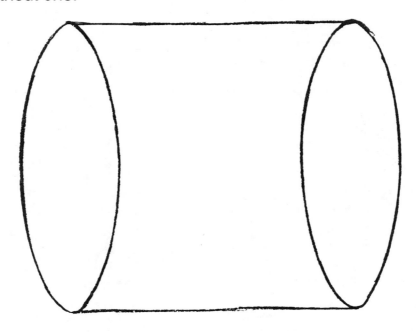

Here comes the magic part: you can carefully erase one little line in your drawing and make it look like this:

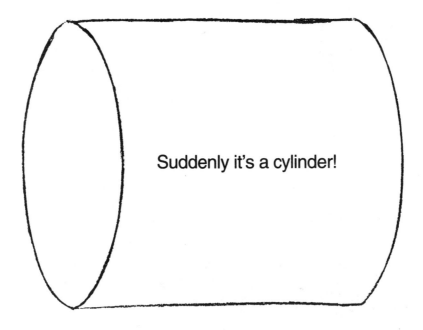

Suddenly it's a cylinder!

If your first cylinder drawing looks a little, well, *wobbly*, don't be alarmed. You might want to try drawing one on a piece of graph paper, or making yourself some guidelines to follow.

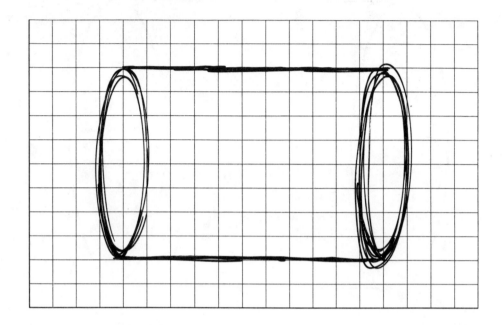

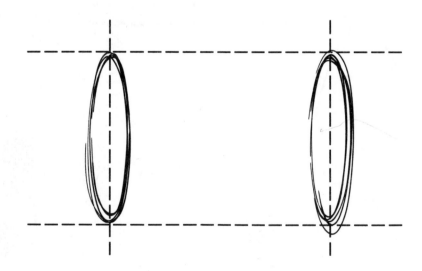

Do whatever works best for you.

Part 2

....

Mysteries Unfolded:
more round stuff that isn't really round

Drawing perfect cylinders may not be easy the first time. Drawing takes practice (remember trying to ride the bicycle?). You might find that two ellipses you draw aren't exactly the same. Or your cylinder might not look like it's standing up correctly.

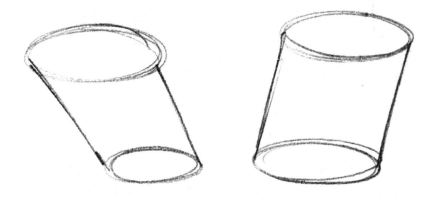

Actually, both the 'mistakes' above are still perfectly good drawings. They're just not perfect cylinders—in fact, they're more complicated than simple cylinders. In this section, we're going to try drawing some cylinders that aren't proper cylinders—not like the ones above, perhaps, but we'll discover that you can change parts of the cylinder and it becomes—different. You'll see. Grab your pencil and paper.

Start by lightly drawing an ellipse, just as before.

Strategy #2

• •

Do you remember what the first strategy was? Do you? Really? If not, turn back to page 13. Strategy #2 won't do you any good without strategy #1. Here's the strategy: be on the lookout for ways to turn your paper to make drawing easier. Since it's generally easier to draw a straight line from side to side—rather than top to bottom—be ready to turn your paper sideways any time it might make drawing a line easier. Turn the paper upside–down if you need to. When we write, turning the paper upside down doesn't do a bit of good. Try it when you're drawing a cylinder, though—you'll be amazed!

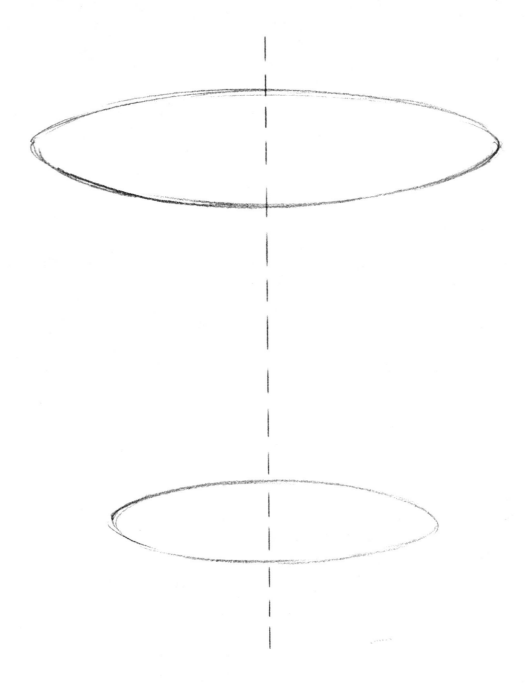

Now add a smaller ellipse directly below the first. (A guide line in the center might help in lining them up.) The bottom ellipse should be the same as the top ellipse—not wider or thinner—simply smaller!

Now turn your paper sideways (remember our strategy for easier straight-line drawing?) and connect the ends of the ellipses.

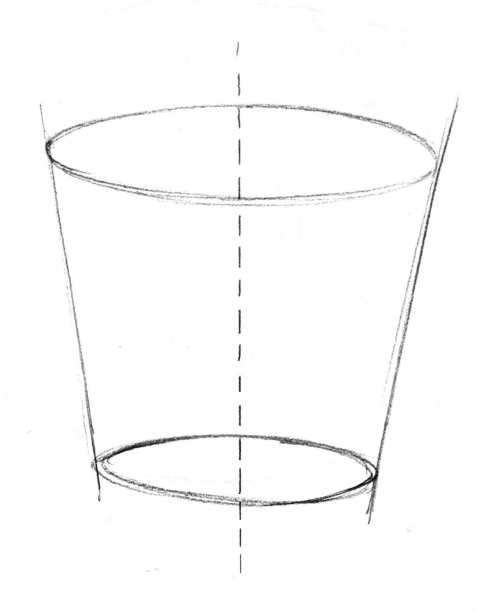

Here, complete with guidelines, is the whole drawing. If yours doesn't look like this, **compare** the two closely—look at the **angles** on these guide lines. Are both sides of your drawing the same? Is the bottom ellipse directly below the top ellipse?

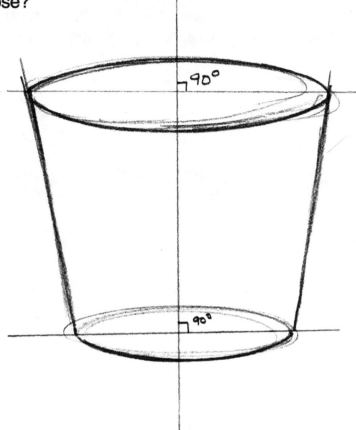

Or, just for fun, look at your drawing in a mirror....

Strategy #3

• •

Get in the habit of looking at your drawing in the mirror from time to time. (Don't forget to smile!) Use the mirror to analyze your drawing: which parts look right? Which parts don't look right? Compare what you see in the mirror with what you see while drawing, and you'll quickly spot mistakes you didn't even know were there!

We've just finished drawing a cylinder with one end smaller than the other. Below is an example of a common object with that form. Can you think of other objects whose form is similar?

Let's step back a moment. Suppose you started to draw the flowerpot shape, but instead of drawing the bottom ellipse, you just continue the sides

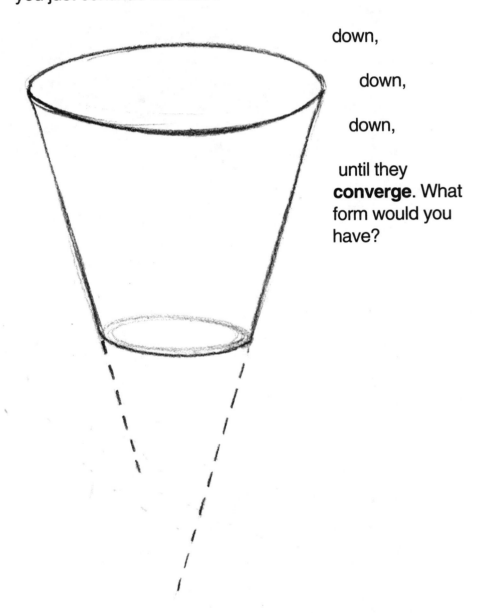

down,

down,

down,

until they **converge**. What form would you have?

It's a cone—just like an ice-cream cone.

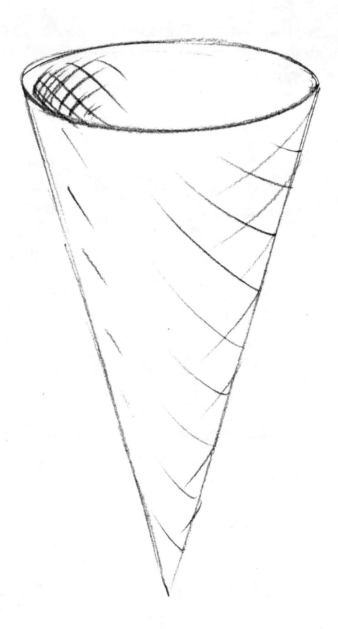

Or a megaphone.

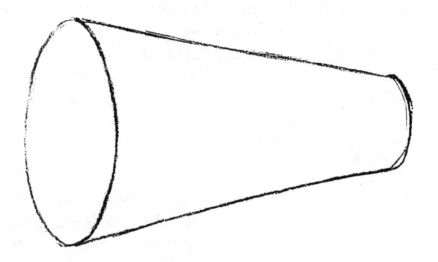

Or a traffic cone.

Remember: when you look at the top of a cylinder, what you see (usually) is not round. Most of the time, because you're looking from an angle, you'll see an ellipse. When you draw a cylinder, it's the ellipses that make it look real.

You can also draw forms that don't have straight sides, or that aren't exactly cylinders—a lantern top, a teacup. Keep your eyes open for everyday objects that contain ellipses, and see if you can draw them. You might be surprised how many "round" things there are around you that aren't round!

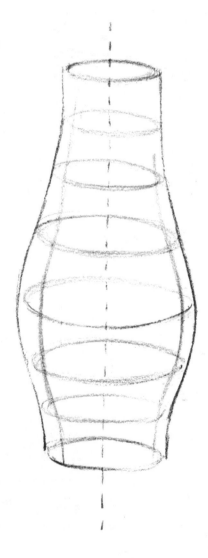

Whenever you have a few minutes, practice drawing cylinders or ellipses. The more you practice, the better you'll get—and they're great starting points for doodles and designs!

Part 3

. . . .

Mysteries of Rectilinearity Revealed:
Your Basic Box

This is your basic box. It's easy to draw (remember the strategy #2 on page 18!). But it's not very exciting. It's just a plain old **two-dimensional** rectangle. To make it to look like a **three-dimensional** box, we need to make it a little more complicated.

(Clues: Lightly. Turn paper.)

Step one in making the two-dimensional rectangle into a three-dimensional box is to draw another rectangle exactly the same shape and size. Place it off to the side a bit, and slightly above or below the first rectangle.

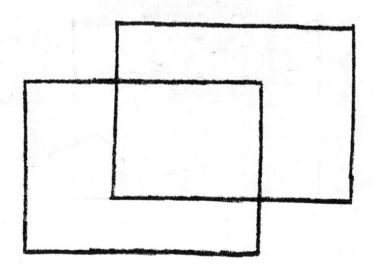

Now connect the **corresponding** corners (upper right corner of first box to upper right corner of second box, upper left corner of first box to upper left corner of second box, and so on). Remember (strategy 2?) to turn your paper a little bit to make the **diagonal** lines easier to draw.

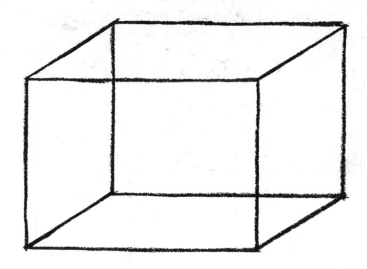

If you've been drawing lightly (as I'm sure you have been, remembering strategy #1...) you can now erase certain lines and make a three-dimensional box drawing that will look like one of these two.

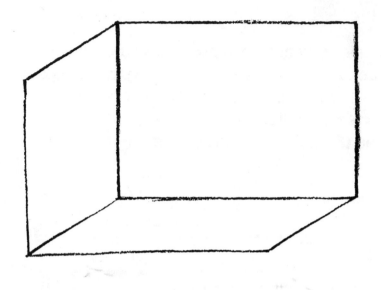

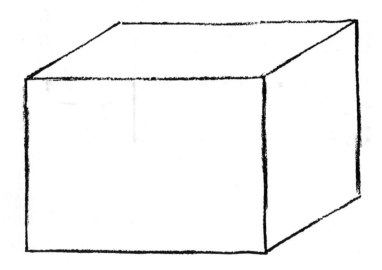

Or, you can leave it like it is and you'll have an **optical illusion**. When you look at this drawing, do you see how it could be either of the boxes on the previous page?

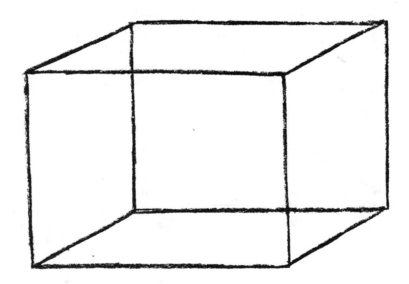

Take a moment to compare the two drawings below. Each is
a box. How is one box drawn differently from the other?

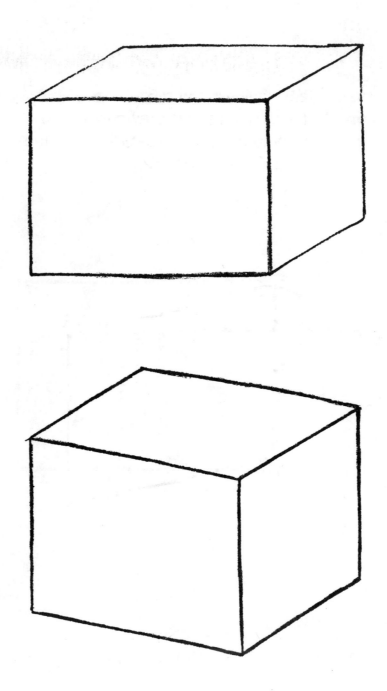

Here's a clue: look at just one side (or face) of the box. The first box has the front face drawn as a rectangle—and there are no rectangles at all in the second box! Instead, in the second box, each face is a **parallelogram**.

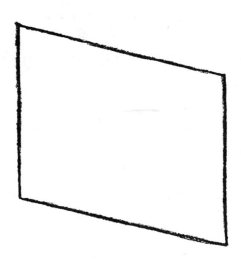

When you see a box in front of you, it usually looks like the second drawing, like this:

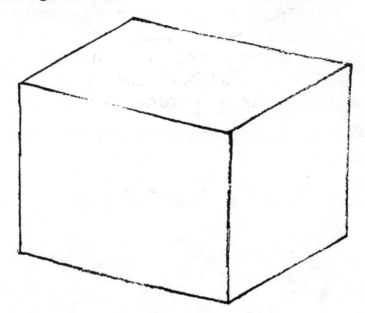

But if you were looking down on a very large building, it might look a little more like the drawing below. How is this drawing different from the one above?

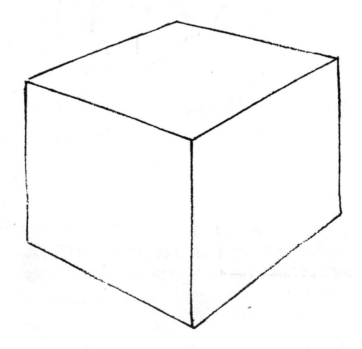

Hint: in the second drawing, imagine the lines on the top and bottom of each face extending until the lines converge at a distant point. This technique is called **two-point perspective**: the lines **converge** on a **horizon**. In this example, you can see the horizon. Sometimes you can't—there might be trees, or hills, or other buildings in the way. The principle, though, is the same.

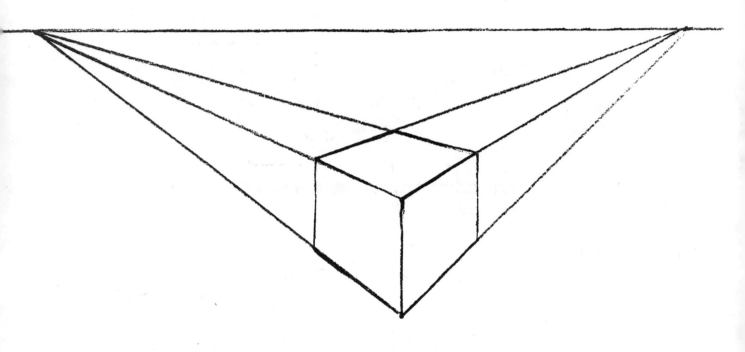

Two-point perspective can be tricky to learn to draw. But now that you know it exists as a drawing technique, you'll be able to spot it in other people's drawings and paintings—and even in photographs. (For more instruction in perspective drawing, see my book *Learn To Draw 3–D*.)

Here are all three types of box drawings together. Can you remember what is distinct in the way each is drawn?

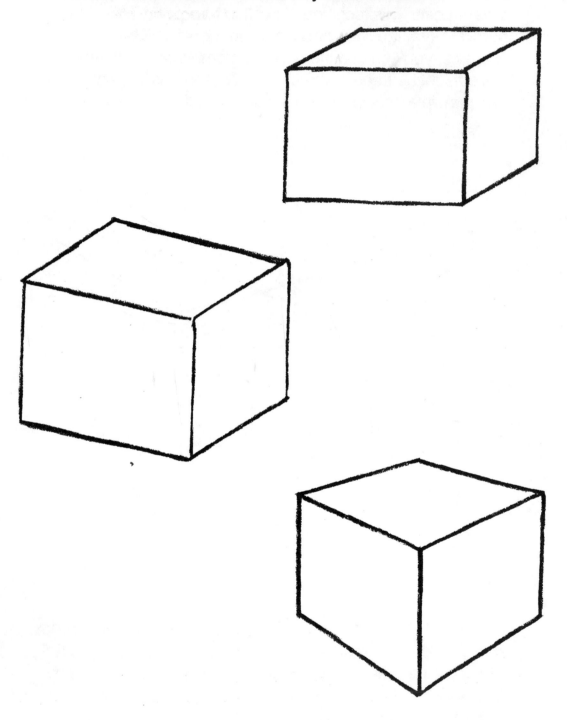

(One of them contains a rectangle. One of them is made up of parallelograms. And one points to a horizon.)

From basic box to basic dwelling

One of the things everybody seems to know how to draw is a house. Let's see how we can turn our basic box into a three-dimensional drawing of a house. Grab a pencil, and a piece of paper, but—WAIT A MINUTE! We can't do anything with this drawing unless we remember Strategy #1 and Strategy #2: what are they?

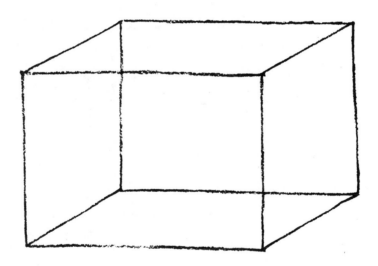

Start out lightly—draw a basic box like the one below. Add little dots to your box where you see them here, in the middle of the bottom of each rectangle, where you see them below.

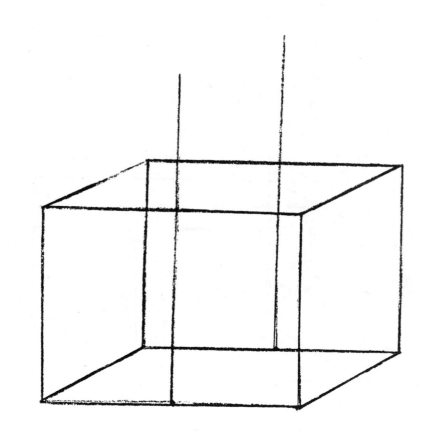

Now turn your paper sideways and extend those two lines—lightly, of course!

Add a line connecting the tops of the two lines you just drew. You can decide how high you want the peak (or top) of the roof to be; just make sure the line that shows the peak of the roof is parallel to the lines of the sides of the house.

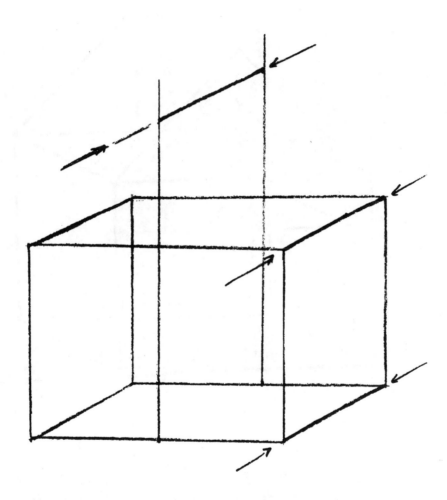

To complete the form of the house, draw lines to connect the peak of the roof with the top corners of the box.

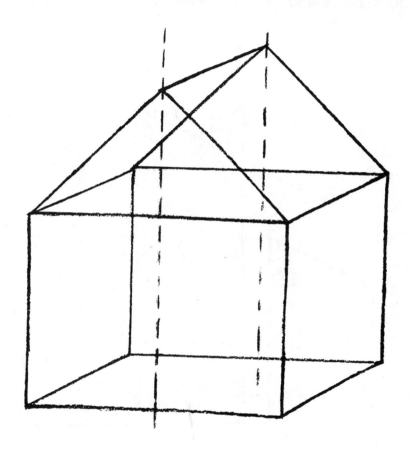

Before you say that yours doesn't look perfect, remember, once again, the strategies that can help you: 1. Start out lightly; 2. Rotate your paper if you need to; and 3. Check out your drawing in the mirror from time to time. If those don't work, there **is** one other strategy—we'll get to it....

This is what the basic house looks like without all the lines used to draw it. When a real house is built, there's a lot of work that gets hidden when the walls are finished. It's the same in drawing a picture of a house!

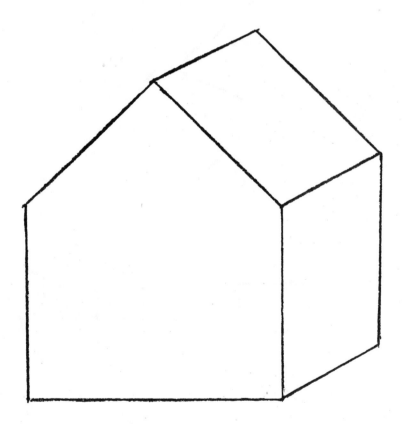

It's not difficult to add windows and a door to the house. The **vertical** lines go straight up and down, as you might expect—but the **horizontal** lines are parallel to the other horizontal lines in the drawing.

The door looks like this:

And the windows look like this:

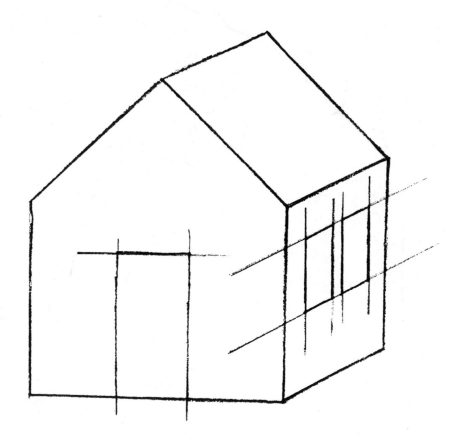

You can add as many details as you want—just make sure you follow the basic rules.

The house we've just put together is based on the first type
of box drawing we did—the one with the rectangle. To make
your drawing more realistic, you might want to try it now,
using the other types of box drawings (remember, the two-
point perspective is tricky—don't get discouraged if you have
difficulty with it!).

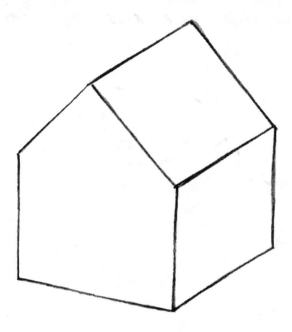

Parallelograms

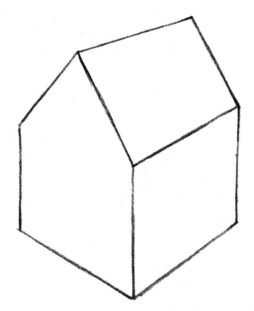

Perspective

Part 4

· ·

Creating a Complete Picture

Look at these two cylinders. One looks closer to you. Why?

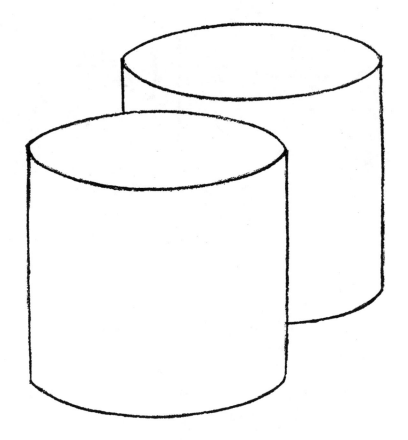

The cylinder on the left looks closer because it covers up
(**overlaps**) part of the other cylinder. This is a compositional
technique you can use to help create a sense of depth in
your drawings.

Look at these two cylinders. They don't overlap, but one still looks closer than the other. Why?

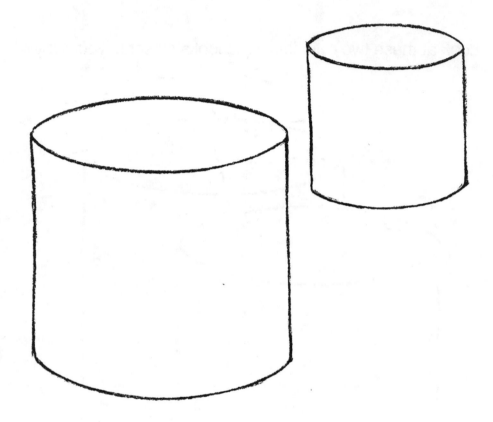

Another easy way to create depth in your drawings is to make objects in the **foreground** bigger, and objects in the **background** smaller.

When you use both these techniques, overlapping and foreground-background, in the same drawing, you can see how easy it is to create a picture that looks like it goes far into the distance!

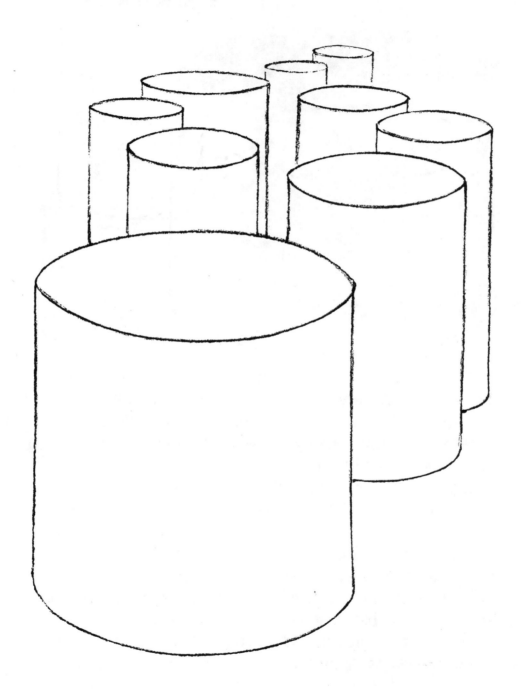

If you like the idea of creating a drawing that makes things look like they're very far away, here's another idea. The air through which you see objects far way is full of dust, and water vapor, and for many of us—unfortunately—air pollution from things like cars and factories. You don't draw the air in a picture, but the air changes the way things appear. When something black is far away, it doesn't look as dark as when it's up close. When something white is far away, it doesn't look as light as it does up close. Everything gets grayer as it gets farther away—it has less contrast. In your drawing, give the objects in the foreground the most contrast—the whitest whites and the blackest blacks—and make the objects in the background get grayer, and grayer, and grayer. This is called **atmospheric perspective.**

The other way artists make things look real is by adding **shading**. In fact, when you draw you can spend hours studying shadows and learning how to make them look real. To get started, though, even simple shadows can help your drawings, and on the following pages are shading strategies.

Strategies for shading, Part 1

1. Hold your pencil sideways when shading.

When you want to add shadows to a drawing, it's easier—and a lot quicker—if you turn the pencil sideways, and use the side of the lead. (Pick up the pencil as though it were a knife on a dinner table, as though you were about to butter a piece of bread. Then put one finger near the sharpened end. Move it from side to side on the paper, and you'll get a nice broad, gray mark.)

2. Follow contours.

Shading usually involves lines of some kind. To make a drawing look real, it helps to have these shading lines follow the **contour** of the different objects. On a cylinder, you can follow the elliptical curve of the top or bottom, or you can follow the edges, which are straight lines. Or both.

Remember to turn your paper around—even upside down!—if that will make any part of the drawing easier.

3. If it doesn't look right, try adding more shading.

Don't be afraid to ruin a drawing or two by over-shading. You need to learn for yourself how much shading you can add. Experiment—it's the way you'll find out what looks best.

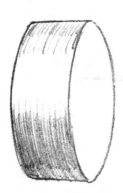
Contour shading lines

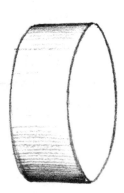
Straight shading lines

Combination of both

1. Decide where the light is coming from.

In order to have shadows, there must be light. And that light must come from somewhere. Natural light usually comes from one general direction—above, above to the right, above to the left—and causes shadows in the opposite direction (below, below to the left, below to the right). If you make a straight line from the light source, through the object, it leads to the shadow—when there's something like the ground for the shadow to fall on.

Can you figure out where the light is coming from in each of these drawings of a **sphere**?

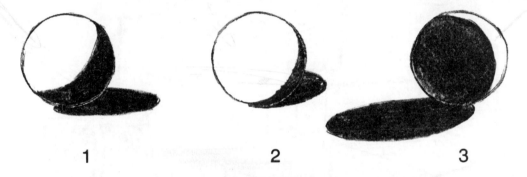

1   2   3

2. Realize that the light source does not need to be in the picture.

If we walked outside in the middle of the day, and I said, "Look at my shadow," you'd probably look down at my shadow and not see the light source. The sun would be overhead somewhere. You could look at the sun, and you could look at my shadow, but it would be difficult to see both at the same time. If you drew a picture of me (and my shadow), it wouldn't make much sense to add the sun. In the middle of the day, you simply wouldn't see both at the same time. (Unless, of course, you happened to be in Fairbanks, or Reykjavik, or Helsinki, or Yakutsk, and looking south.)

The drawing on the cover of this book contains three forms: a box, a cylinder, and a sphere. We're going to make a drawing that contains those three forms, so if you can find a box, a cylinder (preferably a tin can) and a sphere to look at, that will help.

The drawing here is based on a baking soda box, a can of stewed tomatoes, and a tennis ball. You might not find that exact combination of box, cylinder, and sphere. You might want to try a pile of different boxes—or several different sizes of cans—or a basketball, a kickball, and a baseball. Use whatever you have—the ideas still apply.

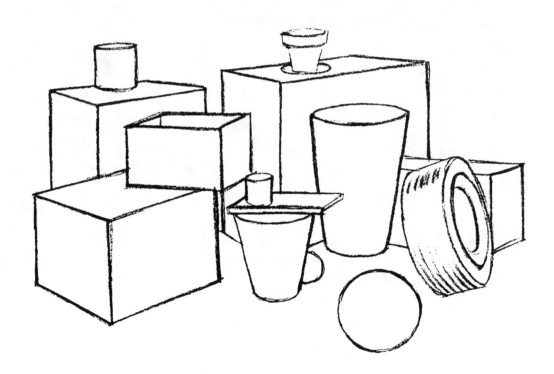

The box should be fairly easy to draw, even if it takes a couple of tries to get it just right. This box has a circle on the side, and you can see we've added some guide lines. The guide lines serve as a reference—they won't be part of the final drawing, but for now they make it easier to get the drawing of the circle just right.

If your box doesn't have a circle on the side, why not add one? Trace something round onto the box, or use a compass—make sure it's absolutely round. Then look very carefully, and try to draw it. Try making your own guide lines, very lightly.

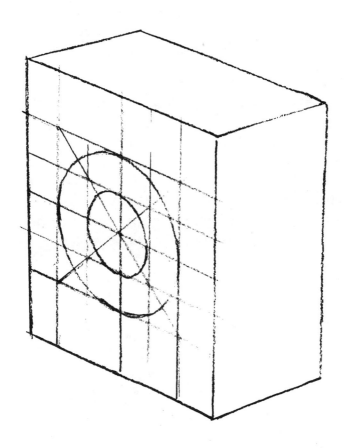

Next observe how any lines or writing on the sides of the box follow the sides you've drawn—EXACTLY. Every line of writing on the side of the box runs at exactly the same angle as the top and the bottom of the box.

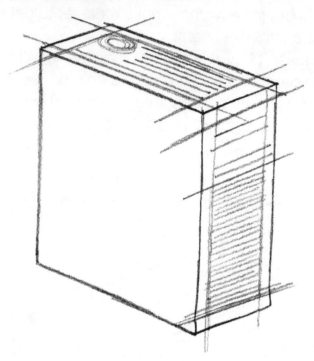

When you draw the printing, you don't have to make all the individual letters, unless they're very easy to read. You can make scribbly marks going up and down, running along your guide lines, and they just might look like the writing on the side of the box.

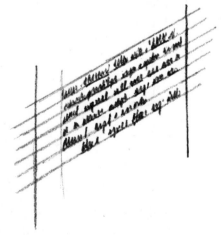

After the details of the box are all drawn, and all the angles are right, then it's time to add the cylinder. In this drawing, the cylinder is in front of the box, and so it's drawn very lightly— as if the box wasn't even there.

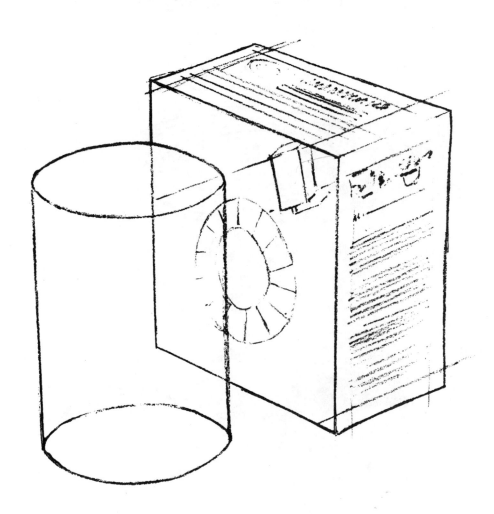

The top of the can is certainly the most challenging part. To make it look real, you can start with concentric ellipses, and then carefully look for shapes of light and dark that fit into them. Add reflections one at a time. You'll notice that the reflections all change as soon as the light source changes, so if you do this drawing in more than one sitting, you'll want to be sure the can doesn't move (or the light source)!

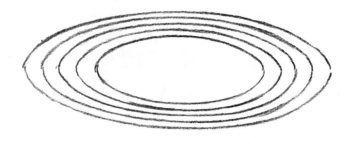

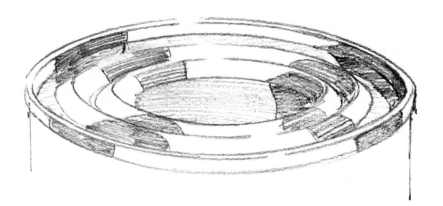

Remember the shading strategies on pages 50 and 51? One of them involves drawing lines that follow contours. Now, as you look at the can, you'll see that the writing on the side of the can curves around it, just as the ellipses of the top and the bottom of the can curve. With lightly drawn curves as guide lines, add the writing. Turn your paper upside down while drawing the curves; make very light guide lines for the smaller writing and fake it, the way we did with the box.

With lines on the can that are diagonal, or curved, you'll simply have to look very carefully and figure out through observation how to add them to your drawing.

When you have the cylinder put together, you can add the sphere. It's easy, because no matter how you look at a sphere, it's always the same shape—a circle.

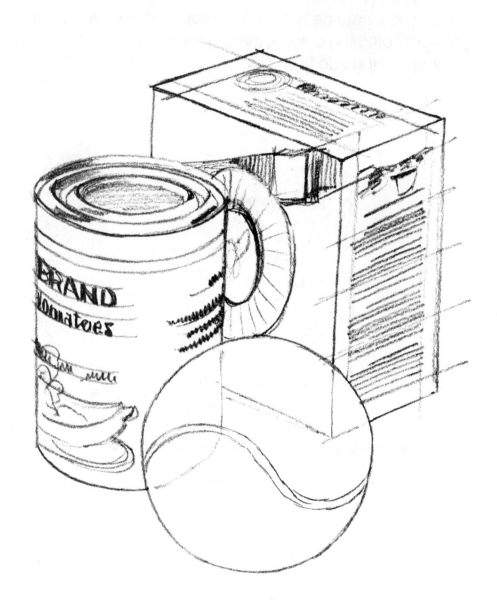

So far, everything in the drawing is still very lightly pencilled in. Now look at everything in front of you, and decide what is the very darkest part of the drawing. Decide which part is the very lightest part of your drawing. And, if you haven't done so, draw yourself a little gray scale. The darkest part of your drawing probably wants to be as dark as the darkest part of your gray scale. The lightest part of your drawing may be just the white of the paper.

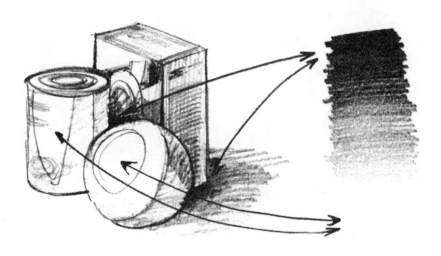

An interesting note: if you took a color photograph of your box, cylinder, and sphere, there would probably be no absolute white or absolute black—everything would have some color. One of the secrets, then, of making a drawing look like a photograph is looking very carefully at all the colors (shades of gray, if you're drawing in only one color) and the areas where they run into each other. In a photograph, too, you rarely see outlines—you see areas of one color (or shade of gray) meeting areas of another color (or shade of gray).

Before you begin shading your drawing, too, you need to think about the light—is the light shining from one source? Is it coming from many different sources?

If you are outside in the bright sunlight, you'll see very sharp, distinct shadows. But if you're inside, with many lights overhead, you may only see very softly defined shadows— lighting for classrooms and libraries, for example, doesn't give many shadows. If you're on a stage, with many spotlights, you'll see many different shadows.

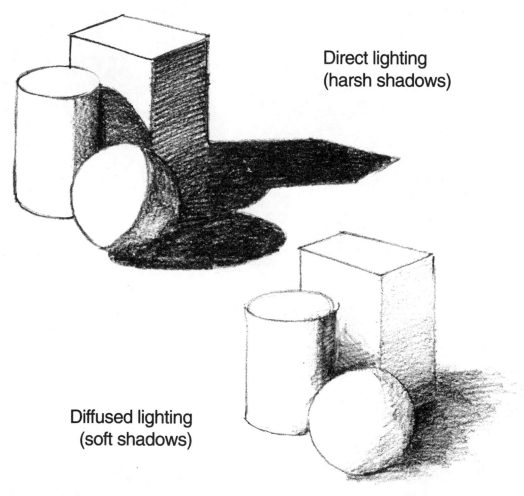

Direct lighting
(harsh shadows)

Diffused lighting
(soft shadows)

There is no right or wrong light for drawing (as long as you can see your paper!). Just observe what light there is, and draw the lights and darks that you can see.

Sometimes it's helpful to do a quick study on another piece of paper. The shapes don't have to be perfect, but you can try out one thing at a time—whether ellipses or, as in this case, shadows. If you draw most of the details first, and then add shadows, you may have to make shadow details darker. Notice here how the curved lines on the can are darker where they are in shadow. Do you notice that in real life? It's a detail in drawing worth watching for.

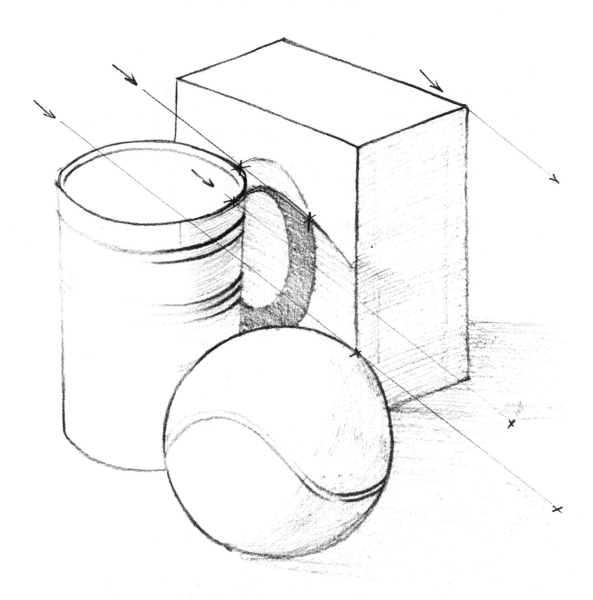

The point of all this isn't to have you copy a picture out of this book. The box, cylinder, and sphere are all easy forms to locate, either in school or at home, and if you can, try to set up a little area near a window where you can practice drawing.

Now that you have an idea how the basic shapes of the box, cylinder, cone and sphere are made, you can draw quite a few manufactured objects you see around you every day: cups, glasses, lamps, plates, tires, trash cans, crayons, doorknobs, wheels, clocks—try drawing them! Practice! Some will look great the first time you try, and some will probably need a few tries before you feel good about them.

Don't rely on others to tell you whether you're drawing is good or not. You know—and they don't—whether you did your best in the drawing. Think about Strategy #3, using a mirror, and if you haven't tried it, do so now! It's like seeing your drawing through someone else's eyes!

When you do a drawing that **you** think is great, congratulate yourself! Good work! Now look for something else to draw—maybe something more challenging, something that **won't** look so good the first time you try it? Always keep your eyes open for new things to draw: you'll never get better if you keep on drawing the same old stuff, over and over and over—always look for new challenges. You won't forget how to draw the old stuff—ever. I promise.

Also, keep your drawings—even if you don't like them at first. Keep all of them. Put dates on everything—later you can be pleased with how much better you've gotten! Make a little folder, or portfolio, to store all your drawings. At some point in the future, you might want to get rid of some, but not until they've had a chance to age a while. Some of them will actually improve, just by sitting forgotten for a period of time!

Here's a simple and inexpensive way to make a portfolio. Make it a bit larger than the paper you use.

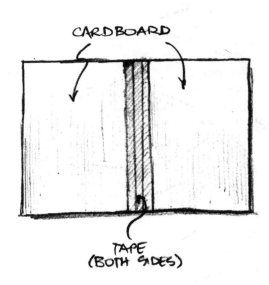

CARDBOARD

TAPE
(BOTH SIDES)

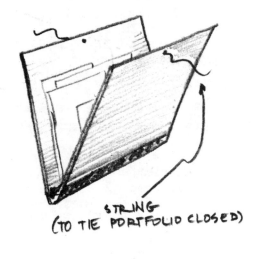

STRING
(TO TIE PORTFOLIO CLOSED)

Final, and best, strategy

· ·

One of the questions I'm often asked is "How do you get good at drawing?" I answer by asking this: How do you get good at playing soccer? How do you get good at reading? How do you get good at playing the piano? Or dancing? The final, and best, strategy, is to

P R A C T I C E !

Index

If you've borrowed this book from the library or a friend, and want your own copy, ask at your local bookstore if they carry it. If not, suggest they do— booksellers often appreciate suggestions from their customers. If that doesn't work, order directly from Peel Productions, PO Box 185-DN, Molalla, Oregon 97038-0185. Please send check or VISA/MC [number, name, expiration date, and signature]: $7.95 per book plus $2.50 for shipping and handling (any quantity). And do tell us where to send the book!